Additional praise for *Dragonfly. Toad. Moon.*

Mary Jane White's *Dragonfly. Toad. Moon.* is a book highly attuned to perception. The poet's intuition and gift for language runs parallel to her neurodiverse son's artistry, the clay he throws becoming "A vase that flows out and, breathing, closes in / Upon what is now a nearly perfect lip." As a mother learns her son's modes of expression, she cares for him with a fierce intelligence and desire to understand his vocalizations that might otherwise go unheard. Dragonfly. Toad. Moon. is a beautifully complex collection. A wonderfully human, humane, and empathetic achievement.

—Denise Duhamel, author of *Second Story*

Mary Jane White describes raising her son with autism the way he and all of us experience our lives—in blinks—sometimes in the moment, sometimes not. She talks straight but underneath the straight is poetry that is all her own. And no matter how difficult things get, you have the sense that in the end, Ms. White's patience and the depth of her love for her boy will prevail. And in three clicks—dragonfly, toad, moon—they do. This is a tender and fearless book.

—Lola Haskins, author of *Asylum: Improvisations on John Clare*

Mary Jane White's *Dragonfly. Toad. Moon.* speaks to the mute heroism endemic to caregiving and to how patience is less a virtue than a survival skill. Deploying an ear honed on the music of Modernist masters, her lyrics oscillate between the sweetly, and sadly, personal and the divinely cryptic, and the current they produce powers a humane, thoroughly adult vision.

—Richard Katrovas, author of *Poets and the Fools Who Love Them: A Memoir in Essays*

D0168073

A child with autism is a mysterious blessing. In *Dragonfly. Toad. Moon.*, Ms. White perfectly captures this. For parents and teachers of these children, this book will be a strong comfort after exhausting and challenging days. I remember my wife and I meeting Ruffin; she, who had never met a person with autism before, remarked, "He seems like a regular child!" Indeed, he did—at five or six, after years of ABA therapy. All the more so that sweet Ruffin changed many lives because Ms. White battled for critically necessary ABA services (woodenly, and like teaching a parrot to talk), and sent out dozens of copies of her efforts to other parents whose sleep-deprived days were filled with experiences similar to those she recounts herein. An inspiring read for all of us and should be required reading for the decisionmakers who impact all the Ruffins in the world. I wept and smiled as I read it.

—Sonja D. Kerr, Connell Michael Kerr, LLP

Writing both as the young daughter of parents and as the ferociously dedicated single mother of a son with autism, Mary Jane White's vivid snapshots, her poems, burn into the mind. A web of knotted string fills a room. A struggling naked boy hurls a curtain rod, makes four empty swings swing together precisely, is swaddled, raging, in a towel. With his mother, we endure horrifying images of children with autism who could not be taught. But then, finally, as the tensions relax, the blessed beginnings of learning. The language of this poetry is as hard-edged and compressive as the images it shapes. The poems are unlike any I have ever seen, as unforgettable in method and content as the story they depict. Had White named her remarkable book with adjectives instead of nouns, she might have called it *Hard. Bright. Fierce.*

—Judith Moffett, author of *Tarzan in Kentucky*

I have spent over forty-five years working with and observing children with autism, their families, seeing how they overcame the difficulties and experienced the emotional significance of this life course. It takes an artist, a poet, to capture the experience, the upside down communications, the anxious expectations. Certainly there can be, after all, the most hoped-for successes, but there is always love.

—Dr. James A. Mulick, Ph.D., Professor Emeritus in Pediatrics, The Ohio State University

Dragonfly. Toad. Moon.

Dragonfly. Toad. Moon.

POEMS

Mary Jane White

Press 53
Winston-Salem

Press 53, LLC
PO Box 30314
Winston-Salem, NC 27130

First Edition

Cover image by Nouveau Deco Arts of brooch
in a private collection.
Used by permission of the owner.

Author Photo by Chip Peterson

Library of Congress Control Number
2022933277

Printed on acid-free paper
ISBN 978-1-950413-47-8

For my son, Ruffin

Acknowledgments

The author thanks the editors of the publications where these poems first appeared, occasionally in different form:

Adelaide Magazine, "Human Meeting: The Power of One and On"

Appalachian Heritage, "Summer: With a Magnet"

Cutthroat, "Ominously & Brilliantly, Questionlessly Happy"

Illya's Honey, "Taoseans, What Barbarians" and "Good Riddance to Those Years"

The Peacock Journal, "How Is It Enough to Say"

The Rockhurst Review, "Dragonfly. Toad. Moon."

The Southern Quarterly, "Rivalry"

"Good Riddance to Those Years" also appears in *The 50th Anniversary Anthology of the Iowa Writers' Workshop*.

"Dragonfly. Toad. Moon.," was first published in *The Rockhurst Review*, noted above, as a long poem containing early versions of "Tantrum," "Wet," "Park," "Sticks & Strings," "Order," "Sleep," "Talk," "Worse," "School," "Friend," "Time," "Home," "Window," "Empty," "Camp," "Zip Line," "Dusk," "Hill," "Patience," "Sport," "Refractory: All Three," "Near," "Wheel," and "Cursor." It was republished online by *Verse-Virtual* in 2017.

Contents

A Note from the Editor

To best tell the story of my journey with *Dragonfly. Toad. Moon.*
is to tell a fable, for the imagined narrative indeed enforces a useful
truth. I will call it "The Reader, the Editor, and the Parent."

The Reader found the story, the occasion of the poetry, and began
to feel. He brought his life with him and projected the pain of the
poetry onto his own circumstance, his own children, as readers
and parents are wont to do. He lingered there until he felt ready
to remind himself to be grateful, and returned the pain back to the
poems where he preferred it live.

The Editor made demands. *This sonnet needs to behave more
like a sonnet*, he said. *The meter here is distracting, it pulls me
from the poem. And the ending is flat*, he went on. The Editor said,
*The reader doesn't know enough here. This is an unreasonable
expectation.*

The Parent could take no more, interrupting him, *Do you
forget what you are reading?* The Parent said *of course* you are
distracted, *of course* the ending falls flat, *of course* these are
unreasonable expectations. And the Parent said, *Do you know
what these poems must be?*

And the Editor found the poems to be as his children, loving
them and desiring what's best without changing who they are,
what they must be.

This is the masterstroke of Mary Jane White: to force a glimpse of
understanding, tiny as it may be, into the helplessness, love, and
fortitude of the life that lived these poems. I can no more iron out
the meter of a line than Mary Jane could request an uneventful
bath or avoid a tantrum. She has braided the tension of my
perspectives as a reader of poetry, an editor, and a parent into a
triumvirate of reluctant dependence; squarely where she intended
me to be.

Becoming a parent was a deliberate decision for me. I did it on purpose. The same is true for Mary Jane. That intent, however, does not mean we were capable of comprehending the result. Poetry, and especially that found in *Dragonfly. Toad. Moon.*, is no different. If you've picked up this book, you've done so on purpose. But, you can't yet know what all you will find within; what it will do to you.

Christopher Forrest
February 22, 2022

Introduction

by Gary S. Mayerson, J.D.

As its title might suggest, Mary Jane White's brilliant collection of poems, *Dragonfly. Toad. Moon.*, is about hope and the opportunity for transformation. The dragonfly starts life as an aquatic nymph. The toad has an equally inauspicious beginning as an egg floating on the water, and has the potential to turn into a prince. The moon, of course, has its phases and transforms ocean tides. If you are a romantic, the full moon also is thought to bring out our best (or worst) qualities.

I have known Mary Jane White for close to twenty years. We proudly belong to a unique club of sorts. Membership in this club involves the daunting, if not Herculean, task of raising a son or daughter who has been diagnosed on the autism spectrum. Hence, the author's dedication of this work to her son, Ruffin.

Mary Jane White's poetry will most certainly resonate with other parents who are members of the club, and it will provide greater understanding for non-members as well. One poem, "Sleep," concerns the untold damage caused by early autism researcher Dr. Bruno Bettelheim, who held out little hope for a good outcome, blaming parents by telling them that their child's autism was caused by a cold and indifferent "refrigerator mother." "Talk" is about the countless hours of therapy that may be necessary to spur expressive language: "And with this he began to speak." "Friend" is about the importance of having high expectations. "Sport" addresses the attraction of people on the autism spectrum to "discrete events," sports activities such as golf, and the avoidance of the social demands that come with engaging in team sports.

In "Cursor," the moon shows up as an inspirational "crescent at his fingertip." In an instant the student becomes the teacher, pressing his mother's shoulders down so that she can see the crescent moon. While parents of neurotypical children might take such an exchange for granted, this is a big deal for children who must "learn to learn." Parents of children with autism rejoice when their children call another person's attention to some environmental event. "Cursor" recognizes that teaching and learning go both ways and that neurotypicals have much to learn from those who are on the spectrum.

The entire world has spent the better part of the last two years struggling to live remotely. *Dragonfly. Toad. Moon.* offers a refreshing and intimate look at the everyday world of autism, demonstrating the power of one mother's relentless and selfless love, and the importance of human connection and acceptance.

Gary Mayerson is the founder of the first law firm in the nation dedicated to the representation of individuals on the autism spectrum, and is responsible for the first autism case to reach the U.S. Supreme Court. He is the author of two books, *How To Compromise With Your School District Without Compromising Your Child* (2004), and *Autism's Declaration of Independence* (2020).

Love is created, hath a sensate name . . .

From form seen doth he start, that, understood,
Taketh in latent intellect
As in a subject ready . . .

Look drawn from like,
*   delight maketh certain in seeming . . .*

Who well proceedeth, form not seeth,
*   following his own emanation.*
There, beyond colour, essence set apart,
In midst of darkness light light giveth forth
Beyond all falsity, worthy of faith, alone
That in him solely is compassion born.

—Guido Cavalcanti, tr. Ezra Pound

How Is It Enough to Say

The wise are not flustered,
With one searching out this or that object
That is truly lost?
Some shuttle, some key, some note.

One remark to bring solace.

How is it ever enough to say
The humane are not melancholy,
When this or that one is clearly both
At some juncture?

How is it enough to say

The bold are not anxious,
When this or that may prove unworthy
To do, actually?
Some venture, some truce, some war.

Tantrum

A practiced love of sameness:
As in this wild flapping and pacing . . .
Grunting is how he speaks to me.
A thing he wants is somewhere
In the world—find it! by
Looking
Everywhere. At all cost, avoid his tantrum.

A persistent love of sameness:
As in never move the salt and pepper . . .
As he does not speak to people, do not move
A thing in his world.
This will avoid his asking
Where?
This will avoid his tantrum.

A *perseverative* love, of sameness:
As in do not change anything . . .
As he does not speak to people, even me,
A thing in his world
He may love—but whom he will avoid,
By looking
Elsewhere. And avoid his tantrum.

Wet

To wash his hair was some danger.
He might thrash the tub wall with his
Head. How hard he hated any wetness,
Or to change his shirt: led me to drip water
   Down his back, on purpose, once. This,
More than once. More than once. I remember:
   Once he cut himself on bottle-glass,
And no more felt the pain than if his blood
   Were water: was how I learned this.
Blood was nothing until its wetness would
   Somehow bother him, and he'd undress.
      To free himself from what?
Nor run for comfort, nor cry, but only wet
Made him complain, return—not the cut.

Ominously & Brilliantly,
Questionlessly Happy

October 8, 1957
North Carolina

I'd have been swinging
Out in *the backyard*
By the humid, piney lumberyard
In Mount Gilead,

Practicing, as I was *sent*
Out after supper to do,
To sing, somewhat eccentrically,
All the words to

Our *America*
The Beautiful, our
Rippling *Star-Spangled Banner*,
Our *Battle Hymn*

Of the Republic, my bare
Toes straining to tip
The top of the ill-leveled oil barrel,
Rust-streaked and *silvery*,

Leaned in, propped
Against the back of our *rental*
House, low and *modern* with its single
Spindly *carport*.

My hard, splayed toes
Brushed down the bronzed
Clover, and its *bees*, pointed and rose,
Dragged back a

Rut in the wet *clay*,
Swept a dusty-blue
Fingernail *butterfly* aloft and up
That'd sipped, or seemed to,

Among the fallen, green,
Prickly *satellites of*
The *sweet gum*. Somehow and keen-
Ly, I felt I was an

American: home-
Made, *bright*,
Pragmatic—solitary and *proud*.
Look up, and right—

To access memory: Four
Then, as winking *Sputnik*
Flew, flashed—passed us over—
Beeping and *quick*—

Ominously, and brilliantly.

Park

My son toddles to four swings,
Pushes them until he brings
Them into a severe alignment that pleases him.

How long his own severity attends him;
How little he notices or cares for other children—

Except their play disrupt his careful pattern
Of empty swing and empty swing,
Of crossing arc and arc of thing
And thing, two pairs doubling

That leaves three other children out,
                              but leaves him sing.

Sticks & Strings

One morning his crib is an open handful of pick-up sticks
Around his fallen mattress. In how many nights?
He has unwound the metal bolts and nuts and washers
And drawn out the several rods that help hold it together.

A waist-high web of string
Meets me this morning, but
Where is he gone now? Sleeping
Or walking with a string's end in his fist?
I see he has walked from doorknob to doorknob
To cabinet door to doorknob to cabinet door, every one on the floor.
His pattern of walking is woven behind him, so hard and carefully knotted
At each knob and handle and drawer pull, there is no advance possible
Toward him. It is a morning's work to undo this
And a tantrum and a resistance not to be
Met with, I hope, too very often.
I hope he does not repeat this,
As I fear he will repeat this.
I do not want to repeat this.

Rivalry

for our mother

Oooh—that bad seaside vacation you spent
Caught in the surf of my warring sisters
(That they were engaged or married was no matter)
I saw you felt again how selfishly we fought

For your regard, your very eye,
Should you turn to exclaim or reply,

Or even back when you read to us, a group
Of four, your eyes lowered to the book,
With Susan, littlest, in your lap;
Mike, aloof, but touching you with his foot;
And Cathy, jockeying your elbow, who is like
You, perhaps . . .
        Even I watched, your distant hawk,
For your wink that meant to me, your oldest—this story
And jealousy, after all, would be beneath me.

Order

We could not go out. He would not dress,
Or be clothed, or stay clothed, or tolerate
So much as a sock, or stitch, or suffer
A single thread to cling upon his skin.
Nor eat, nor let us eat, or sleep,
Either of us . . .

>Having wrestled with *my angel*
>Forty minutes, or more,
>To our mutual exhaustion,

>Having dodged a curtain-rod
>He'd thrown at spear-like
>Speed off a stairway landing,

>My heart pounding,
>And his head soaking wet,
>The sweat of his exertion

>Brought up baby-curls—
>I thought, as swaddling might
>Calm a jittery newborn,

>That same might work
>In this pinch with a still
>Naked toddler: so

>Having done that, I hauled him
>Several blocks, downtown,
>To our Café,
>whose cheerful waitress

>Observed we *must have been*
>*Swimming* . . .
>   It was
>Summer, so I agreed.

>I just wanted to *order*
>Something.

Sleep

I did not sleep. When
That bedtime came and he banged
His crib, paced all night *in there*,
Babbling one syllable *in his trance*,
Happy it seemed to me, but *oblivious*
(I learned—*oblivious*), I read: the stacks
Of books ordered in—in what scrap
Of time—by mail.

Echoing Kanner, Bettleheim wrote:
Mute autism was all the child of the family's
Death-camp atmosphere,
Whose *refrigerator mother*—nice sound
Bite, that!—stands humming in the kitchen
Corner . . .

For such damage done by language
Should Dr. B. not be
Marched out in blindfold?
Sign that he was simple, blind—no,

Enough that he wandered: free to plagiarize
Other subjects, harmless ones,
Old European fairy tales,
And carelessly.

Talk

You cannot imagine what all I heard,
What little got back to me—*Mary Had A
Little Lamb*—and this likely only
A little of all it was, gossiped about
Our single-stoplight, rural town:

Forty hours' work a week, face to face,
Across a red-blue plastic table—*adults
And nothing but a baby* in tiny plastic chairs.

Do this, do this, do this—the clean, clear repeated
Invitation to imitate—and *No!* (this is
Information, child), and again this: *Do this:
Sit, look, clap, touch your nose, your unseen
Ears, pillow, window, color "yellow."*

Fifty-two weeks a year, two solid years
With no Christmas, Easter, summer,
And with this, *he began to speak* . . .

Like a parrot trained to talk
As the evaluating speech clinician carped.

Human Meeting: The Power of One and On

1

The meeting is scheduled in a room set with a few, hard scattered
chairs.
Planned to be a short meeting. Looks to be a strategy One could
meet by
Making it run on for two hours, as One has an iron butt, and is
angry.

2

The meeting is scheduled in a room with air conditioning. Getting
somewhere?
Strategy this time is front-line friendship, and administrative non-
commitment.
One notes a violation of the relevant, niggling rules of changing
fine-print.

3

The meeting is scheduled on their territory, a trailer with a secretary
and copier.
The head of everything and second-in-command are set to watch One
read all
Their paper. Fat man on a tailbone donut. Deadpan, One matches
scrap to scrap.

4

The meeting is scheduled out of town, closer to the source of power
    and money.
Arrangements are circular, in accord with current theory. All agree
    to face
A perfectly ignorant third party. Some sullen, and One confident. Not
    an end to it.

5

The meeting is in the County Courthouse, public, neutral, local
    ground. The elegant
Court reporter takes the hearing down. One testifies, and cries—un-
    comfortable for
Everyone else. Readily admits mouthing fuck to the front-line souls *who*
    fucked it up.

6

The meeting adjourns to conference phone. One thinks better without
    eye contact.
Lower levels weigh in, and are excused to duty. Strategy now: *Give it*
    up: an offer One
Won't refuse: *honey—a quaver—*some way for Some to pass over One
    and On.

Worse

This was training my loved and long-awaited child
Like a seal
            —better by half, with less than
Half a chance, than the alternatives—

Also researched:

                The black-and-white,
Awful documentaries, worse
Than six-year-old, precocious
Elizabeth Bishop's
February, Nineteen-Eighteen
National Geographic:

        A boy with his hands padded in bandages,
        Harmlessly battering his helmeted head
        In care;

        Or the unsocial male and female
        Teens, seated on a common bench
        In summer, oblivious to each other,
        In their large, unlovely adult bodies,
        Gazes averted from each other,
        And from the relentless cameras;

        Or the starched-faced toddler
        First tracing sun-motes in her palm,
        Making an identical gesture in super-
        Imposition—years later—
        No change in her behavior, her solitary
        Leisure in her thirties, in the quiet or noisy,
        Clean or filthy State Hospital—
        Court-ordered *to be no more of* . . .

        Or the young man later busy looping yarn
        To hook in canvas, seated on the common sofa
        At his group home—the ones there are
        So few of . . .

School

Forty weekly hours' healing work was
Better by half than the available alternatives:

Public school authorities wanted
To teach him *sign*—that beautiful,
Fluid language of the deaf, that fleeting,
Moving language drawn upon the air—
Which makes a picture in the mind . . .

Which he could not do, nor
Attend to—when his attention fixed,
But upon a concrete picture, or solid
Things—
                    Nor would he be expected
To speak to *me* that lovely, fluid way
As there was no thought, no plan
To teach his mother to see, or listen,
Or imagine from the air, and after all
We were not deaf—

                              Yet, out of caution,
I let them take him off to school—
Just three—so they could *play* with him.

A video camera stationed in the dunces' corner showed
He was not prompted to mouth a single word.

                              So when
The stubby bus brought him home,
After six long hours of school,
Two women, in two three-hour shifts,
More on weekends, taught him
To speak our common language, and
How to think in common ways:

Do this, do this, like a puppet, first:
Woodenly—at each request;
Woodenly, at first.

Friend

As woodenly, first, his father sat
Before me in his despair of our ever
Teaching him everything?—when?

     There began to come a few
     Sudden fluencies—until
     He became quietly common
     Over one more year's working time, and
     Entered kindergarten

     Which, of course, was not
     The end of it, as he approached
     Each potential playmate with his
     Single, commanding salutation:
     Friend, Come play with me!
                  not looking
     Up from whatever thing
     Held his fixed attention
               until with further,
     Careful teaching: *Touch Joe, touch Jim,*
     We taught him—from photographs—
     Snapshots arrayed across his desk, each
     Personal name,
             and drummed upon
     The odd, to him, abstract notion
     That in our common world—*Some*
     Will be your friends, and some
     Will not.

Elevator: Standing by a Woman Dressed in Furs

Who could stand near her? And remain unembarrassed? Untouched
By the glint of her diamonds, unmoved by the bright color
And sharp, clean cut of her hair? Uncut by envy,
Or the clean freshness of an un-sweet perfume,
Or greed, or hate? Who could fully eschew evil means?

And would even that be enough for complete virtue?

Time

Then came
Latency: the beautiful, quiet
Years of going back and forth to school,
Simple enough, so:

In science, in school,
I, too, loved repeating it,
The experiment,
A simple miracle:
Crystals growing
Down a string,
Suspended
From someone's pencil:

Down a tall jelly-
Glass, brought
Unbroken
From home—one
Printed with simple
Line-drawn scenes of
Colonial Williamsburg—
Huge, delicate-spoked
Wheels, and passing
Lanterns, a lady's
Piled curls, the jelly-
Jewel backdrop
Eaten up and gone,
So simple—enough:
Solution of sugar
We made
Supersaturate—
Shoveling it in:

        Also into
    Pale iced tea, and
    Clouding each
    Crystal goblet,
    If unreprimanded,
    At the holiday-
    Crowded dining table,

And stirred and stirred
Stubborn sediment
Away to blur—

Time evaporated:
That worked as well
With salt.

Taoseans, What Barbarians

after Cavafy

Have come and behaved so badly
That all these signs are necessary:

On the tribute to lolling friendship
(Three women drenched in color,
Heavy, and heavy-breasted, six breasts
Arm in arm, embracing)—a sharply-
Folded card: *Do not touch this statue*.

Even in the oil-change waiting-parlor
On a lowly, deal and steel-legged table
(Already moved well out of reach
Of any feet) hangs taped an eight-by-ten
Lined notebook sheet on how not to treat
The furniture . . .

And here in Motel 8 (so, not your
Finest 'shabby-chic' but still of low
Compliant adobe)—a securely mounted,
Framed, permanent reminder
To *every* visitor (whether ski bum,
Tourist, gawker, or passing serviceable
Trucker)—*Please be courteous*
Of other guest. (No "s.") *Slamming*
Door and stomping feet (!) *is very*
Disruptive to others. (With an "s.")
Thank you. Front desk.

Home

Back then we saw the house that is our home now. Stepping into
  the car, with a realtor. And pointed it out.
*If I had my choice, I'd make my offer on that one. It. The brick
  mass. On the corner.*
Ah, yes, admired the realtor, *that one will never be for sale.*
And said straight out, *If it were, you could not afford it.*

Then, as life re-righted, when anything could happen again,
I thought, *What else could I make happen?*

My son, then six, went with me.
He said it was *like walking into a church*

Whose interior walls were white. Every wall we saw.

The Creation: After World War II

On our piano, there stood a photograph of our father
As a college-man at Vanderbilt in his roadster—
A long car, with a huge, spiral-wired spare tire mounted on the
    side, behind the door,
So long, the length of the car escaped the picture, as large as it
    was, a full eight-by-ten.
This was the car in which our father courted our mother
    in Nashville.

After they were married, our father drove us as a family.
While our father was at work, our mother drove us—
In her Ford station-wagon—which he had bought for her.
After he married and had children, our father, who loved cars
    and loved to drive,
Only ever bought sensible cars—sturdy sedans, Chryslers, most of them.
Whenever any of the four of his children earned a diploma or a degree
Our mother handed our father his grey photocopy.
At work our father displayed these copies under a banner he programmed
And printed out for himself, probably on an IBM computer—
ALL MY NEW CARS.

This could be just a story. I never actually saw his printed banner.
There was never a take-your-daughter-to-work day in the era
Of my childhood, but, as a story—as I heard tell, most likely
    from our mother—
It told a truth of a kind. If it weren't true, it should have been.
In memory, there remains a world in which it could have been.

Early on, in Presbyterian vacation Bible school, I learned: It was
    not about me,
"Q: Why did God make me? A: For His Own Glory." It must
    have been a good lesson.
It was in the catechism I had memorized. Still, to me, it seemed mean.
God must be smaller-minded than I imagined.

Art was a matter reserved for Sundays. Mostly. Church, the original
    home of art:
Stained glass, organ music, the high rhetoric of the *King James Version*
And the well-prepared sermon. Dr. O'Shields liked to choose a word
    like *agape*
And reason closely upon it: how one sort of love is different from
    another sort
Of love and then another, categorizing, ranking, and summing all
    this up
For the grown-ups, before calling the little children—littler than me—
    forward to tell them a story.

Our whole family would be there. Every Sunday. Without fail. Dressed
    to the nines.
This was our mother's day of the week. On Sunday, we were her family,
Her work on parade. On Easter. And every Mother's Day with
Each of us wearing a red rose secured with a dangerous straight pin
To signify that our mother was living. Our mother with her red rose.
Our father with his red rose. Extending our condolences—with Dr.
    O'Shields—
To all those pinned with a white rose to remember their mothers
    in Heaven.

Window

Second visit: we got no further than the glazed-over terrace at
  the back door.
The woman of the house could not walk and was seated there.
Surgery on her heel.
We glimpsed a dining room, behind the man of the house. He was
  very gracious, of course, but unyielding.
So wonderfully solicitous of his hobbled wife.

Third visit: my son and I stood under a low stucco outcropping—a
  second floor nursery, as it turned out, supported by two limestone
  columns—ornamented, but unclassically—carved with a double
  band of tulips:
A band of buds, below a band of stone, open cups.

We walked through the whole house, once,
Once, room after room, all white, all with stunning windows . . .

Of metal bar, each bore a central medallion—more tulips—bound
  by a narrow, narrow border of green-acid glass:
Crackled clear glass that looked like winter ice, or falling rain.
And sleet, a pebbled opalescent white.
A bronzed opaque black.
A little real green,
A little pale yellow.

To Herself: Concerning Odysseus

And what shall I do with you—

Now that you are sixty: your mind
Seeming to slip in memory, back
To other women, to places I have

Never been?
              Now that—after
Twenty-whatever years—you speak . . .

As if I am called to remember
All these—yours—as one among sisters—
Called to slip back among the livestock

And lost pets of your boyhood?

Empty

Then it came to us, *our white elephant.*
It came as four apartments. My son and I could only afford to live
  in one of them—downstairs.

My son slept in the library, a north room with no closet.
I slept in the original kitchen, another north room, without heat.

Its attic—crow's nest—was empty.
The maid's room was occupied—*Do Not Enter*—my renter's storage
  flickered under a loopy neon ring, serviced by a run of stapled conduit.

My son, my renter, and I were in the basement, waiting out a tornado
  warning. I opened the subject of buying a house—her own home.

Then it was empty enough to touch, to enter the master bedroom
  and linger before the octagonal bay of four double casements, twin
  to a formal dining room below.

My son wants this room. I want this room. It is becoming our
  house now.
We do not always act as if we were in church.

Camp

My twelve-year-old walks into his summer dorm room at physics
   camp. He is sullen. He says it is an ugly room. It is.
He needs to live here, *just a week.*
He appeals to me pointedly: *It only has white walls.* This is an
   argument he's heard, and knows should sway me.
They might have put a little color into it.
I sit on the hard, small bed. To talk.
I say everyone who moves into a dorm moves away from home.
I suggest now he could *buy posters?*
He doesn't care to.
I suggest his roommate might bring posters.
I remind him he will *only sleep here.*
I insist it will be dark then.
He is not philosophical.

Summer's End

My twelve-year-old and friend are camped on the second-story
  side porch, with cats.
They are eating up there. They have even dragged up the cat bowls.

Also, a spool of kite string, and their colored plastic wheels, with
  snapping plastic sticks.

One end of string loops down, across the yard, to a fence.
There is an elegant second string attached, to facilitate retrieval.

All afternoon the plastic wheels of a changing contraption travel back
  and forth, up and down, the singing string they call their zip line.

Dusk

There are no proper places in this house for televisions.
All the proper places are taken by fireplaces.

I take down our latest volume, to read a chapter aloud to my son
   and his fidgeting friend.

Now that the renter's entry is closed up,
Now that the stairwell is opened,
Now that the hallway is free of odd doors,
Now that the doors are back in their appointed places, and open,
Now, anywhere I choose to sit in this house, *I can see out the*
   windows of other rooms.

Living room—sitting by the south wall's fireplace, my eye travels
   easily out the north windows of the library—to the cool, purple
   rhododendron, each spring.
From the dining room's octagonal bay—low sun strikes the tiny, red
   iridescent corners of a sideboard's glazed upper cabinet doors.
Above a table, the central white petal of each glass tulip glows—a
   steady white flame—as the sky darkens.

At dusk, the glass becomes, burns opaque.
This is dinner hour, on the western prairie.

Hill

As I wrote, *this was latency.*
                              And then, he
Was never going to learn to spell, although
We spent every breakfast working at it.
Dyslexia—another awful word,
But more common—intervened:

> At twelve, just past Christmas, at the age
> English cabin-boys signed on
> The Royal Navy, the age—we researched it—
> Marquette left his wilderness home
> For college, for Quebec—
> He moved away to board in Massachusetts.

> I drove to see him, once or twice a month.

> Two years' school, in blazers and khakis,
> And school-colored ties, he learned to listen
> To his laptop computer read for him,

> And how to talk—slowly, in phrases, please—
> Into his headset microphone so his own
> Words would rise up in seconds flat
> Upon his steady laptop's screen: he learned
> To mimic Steinbeck and Hemingway, and
> To print his papers, by pressing *Print*,

> And learned to ski—a flashing solitary—
> Down night-lit Berkshire's Black Diamond Trail,
> To hike Monadnock, and the gentle Linden Hill.

Summer: With a Magnet

We dredged the roadside dust
For iron filings, for hours.
Fringe to a blackened finger.

The boy next door drank kitchen cleaner
And had to have his stomach pumped.
This happened also to each of us—once.

I ate Drano.
Cathy, aspirin, a bottle's worth.
On the screened-in porch, baby Susan

Was bitten through her baby finger by a beetle.
We battled with wet brooms against the wasps.
Our mother claimed I wasn't like to die

When Mike had only broke my vein.
Trains whistled by. The vapor trails
Of planes crossed the sky and one another.

The storms swept over.

Patience

You were born
A girl-child
To grow into
This Christian name,
Which will be
As a shell
To the tender foot
Of a snail; in it
Your heart will
Go on beating
And glistening.

After the cards
Are all fallen
Into their
Rightful places,
After the pure
Accident of
A shuffle,
You will see
The hearts
Line up
With the hearts;
The spades,
With the spades.

Then persist
In nothing:
Water will erase
Your name, your
Heart. Wind
Will carry you
Away. Everyone
Who ever loved
Or remembered
You—though
They persist,
Or do nothing—
Will follow
Or go before you,
The same way.

Sport

        Away,
He learned to play
Within a baseball team,
The year his teachers'
Favorite, unfavored
Boston Red Sox,
Won The Series.

Baseball and golf(!) became
His own preferred, predictable
Games of discrete events:
Do this, do this: these allowed
Him ample room for individual
Acts, feats of skill,
                    while avoiding still,
And still ignores, the social fluidity
Of soccer, or basketball.

Refractory: All Three

A Benedictine wearing a teal-blue and yellow, short, down-jacket,
And below that, a black scapular, his fore-apron and back-apron,

And the brisk skirt of his cassock. A blue and rather chunky bicycle
Propped at the innermost, blue door of the courtyard. Another

Unmoved bicycle with wide-winged handlebars in the monks-only,
Quadrangle garden, into which we may only, but openly, gaze:

These are The Rule's customs of privacy and un-simple welcome.
Our square refectory table placed at a window that opens onto

The dead garden. Our son, their student, and we, are here—are guests here,
And this is their hospitality: Order, Benedictine of the Knights Hospitalier,

Order of St. John of Jerusalem, Order of the Knights of Malta who fled, fled
To the Imperial Russian Navy that extended them all a certain, welcome

Hospitality in the East as Napoleon moved against them. A welcome
Of ancient and heroic tenor: *One who comes so as to please another.*

Near

At fifteen, he is become our perfect scholar,
With good behavior—*yet*—
As caution finds its expression
In this part of the Midwest . . .

He's come nearer home at least—
This warm, odd, dry winter of

> Russet-grey twigs of denuded sumac—uppermost
> Twigs.

> St. Croix, along the Great River, St. Paul, St. Michael, St. Cloud—
> Exits

> Off I-94—the hourly bells—ringing out from Marcel
> Breuers'

> Sculpted concrete banner, spiral back stair, and honeycomb
> Façade.

> Hand-sized pairs of red squirrels' busy to-and-fro pattern:
> Gathering.

> Whether winter proves warm and odd, or dry, the same
> Behavior.

> Dark gray, small, square offset paving tiles everywhere,
> Granite.

> Over these, each weekend, I enter guest rooms of the Abbey
> Monastery.

Wheel

He works his hardest, as he ever has,
Under strict, kind Benedictine tutelage
Of black-robed monks and lay oblates
Near Minnesota's German-American,
God is laughing, St. John's Abbey.
And so am I, as I love, have my living Isaac:

Who is learning ordinary, ancient Algebra,
And new helical, chemical Biology,
Dictating his assigned paper on *Fragile X*—
One genetic disorder I remember
He was tested for—
                    This makes me laugh and sigh . . .

As I am reading him Darwin's
Autobiography,
                in an alcove, Old Seminary:

        As much as ease, as any odalisque,
        His bare ankles, his long feet,
        My down coat—full length—the fat, green sofa.
        Long fingers—cradling a pillow.

        We go back to where he fell asleep . . .
        Don't stop! . . . No, I heard you read that. Leave
        His head lie propped on a cushion,
        Heels—easily beyond now—the other arm's end.

Hell! Greek and Roman history are hard enough
For anyone to dictate well, or spell.

                            Theology is:
Practical lessons in how to make time
For some activity you love.

Ceramics: where he likes most to work,
At length, entranced, seated at the wheel—
Functional, centered spinning, his kicking, kicking
Heel—shaping lightweight cups, a set of plates,
His glazed, shallow dish for loose pocket change,

A vase that flows out and, breathing, closes in
Upon what is now a nearly perfect lip.

*

Good Riddance to Those Years

for James Wright

Eighty, eighty-two, when you and Hugo died,
And Kinnell leaned in and read
From each of you—
And then from Patrick Kavanagh—
Two poems, I remember, and
Can—give me a moment—find:

One, *In Memory of My Mother, so I*
Do not think of you *lying in the wet clay;*
And, *O, commemorate me where there is water*
Which also recalls you in *so stilly*
Greeny at the heart of summer, and even faintly
In the form of address: *Brother,*

And in the description that follows
As a brief disparagement of prose:
A swan goes by head low with many apologies.

Cursor

Fall again. We hike on marshland
With his camera. He found
A dragonfly at first,

And then a toad, the exact
Sandy brown of the pathway's
Ground to draw attention to.

Though I missed them,
Digital captures in his camera
Showed me—the dragonfly—

Slow, old, or hurt perhaps,
It crawled, flipped over, righted,
Wandered off into the grass . . .

His toad was hard, solid,
Still and small. Still,
He saw it, and placed it gently

On a bleaching leaf, for *a good*
Background, for contrast,
As if it were the old, green

Screen for our cursor, when
A cursor was how we taught him
What a finger is to do in pointing:

Make a path for the eyes of two,
Or more, to follow. It dawned
On me that night, the first

Time—fifteen—he pressed
My shoulders down to bring
My eyes between the leaves

And turn them toward the moon,
A crescent at his fingertip.
At one, and two, and three,

We'd lost forever that wonted,
Pleasing show of his
Early childish lisp—

His *beetle in a haystack*—
But, O, and yet, had this,
No—*would* find these:

Dragonfly. Toad. Moon.

Afterword

With every dark cloud is a silver lining.

One cannot fathom the fear and despair a parent must feel when told their son or daughter has been diagnosed with autism. *What is autism, how will it affect my child, what can I do to help, do I have the strength . . .*

With despair comes hope; treatments grounded in applied behavior analysis (ABA) have over 50 years of empirical science. Research outcomes suggest children who receive early intensive behavior intervention (EIBI) starting at four years or younger can achieve the following outcomes as adults: 47% achieve normal functioning; 43% make considerable gains with deficits in the use and/or understanding of spoken language; and 10% make no measurable gains.

It takes a unique parent to decide on the path of EIBI. It is a complex intervention that requires significant parent participation. Parents report it's like having another job. The usual course of treatment is three-to-five years—a marathon with life-changing consequences for parents and children.

Some children, like Ruffin, may be born with savant-like skills, but many skills are developed over the course of treatment. Children's IQ can increase 30-40 points. Language and social understanding has the potential to explode. At times, there is an understanding of complex subjects such as robotics, molecular science, aeronautical engineering or chemistry (Einstein) that goes far beyond the ability demonstrated by typical learners. For most, however, the results are not as glamorous. The majority of children with autism who receive EIBI will make gains, but will not "catch up" to their typical peers. Most children in the "non-best outcome" group will need life-long custodial care, and the parents of these children will live their lives worrying about their children, particularly about when they pass, and the "children" are left to survive without them.

I would like to offer a special thank you for Mary Jane White, though not for her dedication to helping her son Ruffin, which is remarkable, to say the least. I would like to thank her for continuing to advocate for the field of applied behavior analysis long after her son recovered and lives as a fully functioning adult. Parents who continue advocating for autism treatments after their children are finished with ABA hold a special place.

Erik Lövaas
Founder and CEO
The Lövaas Center US
The Lövaas Center Spain
Fundación Erik Lövaas para El Autismo Spain

Notes

"How Is It Enough to Say," page 3: The three italicized lines come from Book Nine, XXVIII of *Confucius: The Great Digest, The Unwobbling Pivot, The Analects, Translations & Commentary* by Ezra Pound (New Directions, 1951).

"Wet," page 5, warps a sonnet-stanza form from the longer poems of John Donne.

"Ominously & Brilliantly, Questionlessly Happy," page 6: The title derives from a critical description of someone lost to memory as penned by Helen Vendler. The constraints of the poem are syllabic. Mount Gilead, N.C. is where our father was banished from IBM's hub in Charlotte by Mr. Stonecipher, a supervisor he had somehow offended. Our father was sent to service a remote territory of small business machines and typewriters in the rural pinewoods. That was how we—my mother, my father, and my little brother, Michael—all wound up in Mt. Gilead with its brick Protestant churches, its box factory, and its single outpost of Charlotte sophistication, Belk's, up a broad wooden staircase over a hardware and dry-goods store on the ground floor.

"Sticks & Strings," page 9, is my homage to the work of the English metaphysical poets (1600-1690) including George Herbert's poem "Easter Wings."

"Worse," page 16: The four final stanzas describe scenes from Dr. O. Ivar Lövaas's classic 1987 video "Behavioral Treatment of Autistic Children," now available on YouTube at https://www.youtube.com/watch?v=oGhIcAnBQZ4.

"Friend," page 18: Joe is Joe Gavin, Ruffin's life-long best friend, who also appears in "Summer's End" and "Dusk." Jim is Ruffin's father.

"Elevator: Standing by a Woman Dressed in Furs," page 19, also derives from Book Nine, XXVI of *Confucius: The Great Digest, The Unwobbling Pivot, The Analects, Translations & Commentary* by Ezra Pound (New Directions, 1951).

"Taoseans, What Barbarians," page 22: A poem of gentle pique for my now very dear community of women-poet-friends in Taos: Lise Goett, Catherine Strisik, Veronica Golos and Leslie Ullman, written as I ruminated over my first unsettling visit to Taos and C.P. Cavafy's "Waiting for the Barbarians," from *C.P. Cavafy: Collected Poems*, translated by Edmund Keeley and Philip Sherrad (Princeton University Press, 1975).

"Home," "Window," "Empty," "Summer's End," and "Dusk," pages 23, 26, 28, 30, and 31: These are all set in The O. J. Hager House , a National Historic Register property. Built from 1907 to 1908, the Hager house is the only known Iowa commission for Chicago architect Robert Clossen Spencer, Jr. who played a leading role in the development of the Prairie School movement in the Midwest, and who wrote the first critical appreciation of Frank Lloyd Wright. The Hager house was designed in what is thought to be the most innovative period of Spencer's career.

"Camp," page 29, recalls Ruffin's summer experiences at the Wisconsin Center for Academically Talented Youth and The Belin-Blank Center at the University of Iowa.

"Hill" and "Sport," pages 32 and 36, are set at Linden Hill School founded by George and Penny Hayes in 1961 as the nation's oldest junior boarding school for boys with language-based learning disabilities. Ruffin attended the last semester of seventh grade and eighth grade there in Northfield, Massachusetts where he was twice awarded The President's Education Award by George W. Bush, Rod Paige, and Margaret Spelling, The Peter R. Walter Gentleman's Award, and The Headmaster's Award Silver Bowl.

"Summer: With a Magnet," page 33, is set in Charlotte, North Carolina where our father was reassigned after training on the IBM 360 in Poughkeepsie, N.Y., readmitted to the good graces of IBM's regional hub.

"Refractory: All Three," "Near," "Wheel," and "Cursor," pages 37, 38, 39, and 42, are set at St. John's Abbey, Collegeville, Minnesota a Benedictine Catholic community where Ruffin attended their rigorous boarding high school, St. John's Preparatory.

"Good Riddance to Those Years," page 41, commemorates poetry readings at The Iowa Writers' Workshop.

Additional Acknowledgments

It takes a village, of course, to raise any child anywhere at any time. To raise a child through a recovery from autism and to further accommodate that child to dyslexia takes the building out of a virtual village across a nation—where some will be your friends, and some will not.

Of those who were our friends, whose lives changed ours for the better, we continue to celebrate these in bright memory: Dr. O. Ivar Lövaas of UCLA's Early Autism Project, Dr. Tristram Smith, his then-recent graduate student in 1994 just beginning his own teaching career in Iowa, and Dr. Bernard Rimland of the Autism Research Institute in San Diego.

Also, some bright stars closer to our own horizon: The late Sue Baker, Iowa's longtime state autism specialist at University of Iowa's Hospital School, who although constrained in her powers, offered good advice under the table; the late Joyce Haas and her husband Doug Haas of Waukon, who accepted Ruffin as a toddler into their home daycare whenever I was summoned into court; and the late Rose Ward of Waukon, who lifted the burdens of housework and cooking until Ruffin was nearly seven.

Also a fallen star lost to us, my baby sister, Susan McDonald White, a fine artist, sculptor, and art conservator who sent us many useful gifts to help teach Ruffin the critical skill of pretending.

Of those who remain our friends, to whom we can continue to express gratitude, these deserve their accolades:

Dr. John-Peter Temple, pediatric neurologist of The Gundersen Clinic, LaCrosse, Wisconsin who made his diagnosis early enough to allow for success in Ruffin's treatment. Dr. Temple eventually wrote the pivotal prescription for Ruffin's ABA instructional treatment.

Other members of Gundersen's autism clinic, Dr. Cheri L. Webb, Kevin Josephson, M.S., Dr. Patricia A. Kondrick, Fran Kakuska, SLP, CCCC, Dr. Larry S. Goodlund, and Dr. David E. Palm also agreed to support ABA as "appropriate," well into its second year, as did an earlier independent autism clinic team of evaluators at the University of Iowa, led by Dr. Al Marshall, including Dr. Betty Simon, Becky Vilda, SLP, CCCC, Dr. Joseph Piven, Dr. Sharon Koele, Beth Vanzee, MSW, and Deb Scott-Miller.

Dr. Glen Sallows of the Wisconsin Early Autism Project offered an early complete case review and written second medical opinion.

Dr. Doreen Granpeesheh, founder of The Center for Autism and Related Disorders (CARD), Autism Society of America Professional of the Year. Born in Tehran, schooled in England and Switzerland, she came to Los Angeles in 1979 where she graduated high school and entered UCLA at sixteen. There she trained for a dozen years under Dr. O. Ivar Lövaas who served as her thesis advisor. As a practicing clinical psychologist and extraordinarily successful entrepreneurial founder of CARD in 1990, by 1994 she was an active researcher and practiced translator of academic research into the field. With her travelling senior therapist, Evelyn Kung (also trained at UCLA), she designed the individual, early, intensive 28-month long program of applied behavior analysis (ABA) as prescribed by Dr. Temple for Ruffin.

Donna Schmidt—part Native-American, half-Norwegian, with blue eyes and brassy blonde hair, all kinky around her round and friendly freckled face, a large presence, jovial, commanding in a rough, but warmly-evolved motorcycle-mama way, a dear friend, and as nearly Ruffin's second mother as anyone—and Lisa White Murphy, her friend, smaller, quieter, as deeply rooted in our small community as anyone, a long-time, trusted daycare provider. When Lisa smiled into the face of a child, her nose wrinkled, and her eyebrows winged upward like a bird leaving a branch. Donna and Lisa came to their work with Ruffin as two women with no experience in special education. Together, Donna and Lisa carried out Dr. Granpeesheh's and Evelyn Kung's plans rigorously and faithfully in all weathers.

Teacher RoJene Beard and special education teacher Pine Wilson of nearby Decorah implemented Dr. Granpeesheh's plan to integrate Ruffin with typically developing playmates over the summer of 1995.

Our local school district's special education teachers, Patricia Novak and Dee Blanchard, and teacher's aide Sharon Walleser, who together with our local regional special education consultant, Marcia Boberg from Decorah were all constrained in their powers, but offered their best special education efforts day-by-day, close to the ground, to Ruffin and me under all the administrative radar and noise of mediation and litigation.

Also, Mrs. Wonderlich's junior high school classes of volunteers who came to my home-office during Ruffin's early years to learn filing and copying, where they found much work to do, and brought flowers and much laughter.

Lois Fergus, an assistive technology specialist at the YMCA in Cedar Rapids, Iowa, who suggested when Ruffin was three that I buy him a Macintosh computer to run special education software programs to support his language learning.

St. Patrick's Catholic School Board and principal Peter Smith offered us a welcome respite from sharp and recurring early conflict with our local public schools and regional special education authorities by sheltering a Waukon Nursery School's class taught by Karen Perry, and by offering K-8 small-size classes of 10-12 students, promoted as single groups along with their teachers over a succession of two-year periods—a small, stable and kind educational environment with after-school care that let Ruffin grow and thrive.

Dr. Kenneth Olson, our family doctor, Dr. Michael Funk, DDS, our special needs dentist at Gundersen, Pastor Larry Olson of First Presbyterian Church, an exceptional parent himself, as well as Ruth Lembke and Diane Rissman of our local autism support group in northeast Iowa, who organized auditory integration training (AIT) to be provided by practitioner Lisa Tolson to four of our children with autism in the summer of 1995.

Robin Ouren came to watch and write about AIT for the newspaper and stayed to become my secretary.

Andrea Shelton, who later replaced Robin, from the unfailingly kind members of the Shelton family at Jadecc's Copy Center (who ran many free copies to be mailed): Corey Shelton, the late Don and Judy Shelton, and their daughter-in-law, Lisa Shelton, SLP, who expertly finished off Ruffin's Lövaas program during latchkey aftercare at St. Patrick's Catholic school.

Jan Newmann, Ruffin's advocate in county case management, smart, empathetic and one who smoothed the way for many of us.

As I ran into a brick wall of public school resistance, Attorney Curt Sytsma and his paralegal Joan Hannum of Iowa Protection & Advocacy Inc. of Des Moines accepted Ruffin's *Individuals with Disabilities Education Act* case, and drove it unerringly as their vehicle to establishing higher legal standards—resulting in more frequent provision of year-round special education for all students with disabilities in Iowa—bringing in a 1996 decision rendered by Dr. Susan Etscheidt, our state's administrative law judge.
See: https://educateiowa.gov/sites/files/ed/documents/book13dec218.pdf

Attorney Scott Peters of Council Bluffs and Jane Zanglien of Texas assured that Prudential Insurance would reimburse their fair share of the costs of Ruffin's treatment.

Attorney Beth Hansen of Waterloo. "Beth The Good" to my mind, eventually counseled our local school district to reimburse their fair share of Ruffin's early treatment in mediation, and after losing the 1996 due process case our district pressed her to defend before Dr. Etscheidt, gracefully and effectively advised her clients to reconsider any further opposition and agree to advance their fair share of the costs of Ruffin's continuing private school education through middle school and high school.

Attorneys Mark S. Soldat and Don Thompson, my trial partners, who took up the slack when I needed to be home, and judge Stephen P. Carroll who ordered I might continue to work from home during Ruffin's early treatment.

Exceptional parents: Rick and Diane Wenndt, Dr. and Mrs. Raul Espinosa, Attorney and Mrs. James Carfagno, Jr., Dr. K. G. and Mrs. Woodward, Michael and Chris Foster, Michael and Susan Smith, Samantha Johnson. Attorney Bonnie Yates, Attorney Valerie Vanaman, Allison Hanken, and countless others who offered support through our list-serve, The Me List.

Regional and state allies Marion McQuaid, Mark Monson, Dee Ann L. Wilson, a state mediator, Gerry Gritzmacher, who sometimes wavered, Dr. David Bishop of Luther College, who never did, and his student Angie Robeson, who spent the summer of 1996 with Ruffin at Decorah's Sunflower Daycare Center carrying out Dr. Granpeesheh's prescribed program for preparing Ruffin for mainstream integration before he entered kindergarten.

National parent and professional allies: Dr. Ron Huff, Linda Mayhew, Attorney Katherine Dobel, Attorney Mark Williamson and Attorney Ken Chackes.

Iowa Vocational Rehabilitation as established under *Section 504 of the Rehabilitation Act* and counselors Curt Jones, Mindy Meyers and Steven Lieberherr.

Shelly Lacy-Castelot, independent educational and assistive technology consultant who expertly assessed Ruffin's dyslexia mid-way through seventh grade and recommended early voice-recognition and optical character recognition software.

Summer Science, Technology, Engineering and Math (STEM) camp teachers Gary E. Glenn (Computer Graphics/Animated Figures), Lyle Litchey (Building Radios), Don Brauhn (Everyday Physics for the 21st Century) at the University of Iowa's Belin-Blank Center, teachers Doug Richardson (Rocketry 101) and Matthew Goodman (Not Quite C) at Iowa State University's Explorations! and Operation Catapult at Rose-Hulman Institute of Technology.

I will always be deeply grateful to autism authors, researchers, and advocates: Reed Martin, J.D., Pete Wright, J.D., Dr. Michael D. Powers, Dr. Bernard Rimland, Dr. Stephen Edelson, Dr. Dorothy Beavers, Dr. "Catherine Maurice," Dr. O. Ivar Lövaas, Dr. Tristram Smith, Clara Claibourne Park, Dr. Fred R. Volkmar, Dr. Leo Kanner, Dr. Hans Asperger, Dr. B. F. Skinner, Michele Dawson, Nancy Dalrumple, M.S., Dr. Temple Grandin, Donna Williams, Dr. Guy Berard, Anabelle Stehli, Dr. Christopher Gillberg, Dr. Mary Coleman, Dr. Vijandra K. Singh, Dr. Eric Courchesne, Dr. Simon Baron-Cohen, Dr. Uta Firth, Dr. Deborah Fein, Dr. Inge-Marie Eigsti, and Dr. Marcelo L. Berthier. I am equally grateful to their publishers.

Here is the time to thank my own publishers at Press 53, Kevin Morgan Watson and Christopher Forrest. Kevin committed to this manuscript as a larger project than I submitted it. Chris is the consummate weaver of the backstory of my own childhood into the story of Ruffin's. He is my eight-eyed spider suspended by his own spun thread thirty thousand feet above a misarranged manuscript who could discern its final pattern.

My surviving siblings, Michael Thomas White, a retired electrical engineer from INTEL and Cathy Lynn Graham, M.D., a surgeon and race car enthusiast, are remembered fondly in these poems as the children they were, and here for their inspiring and supporting Ruffin in his scientific career.

Most of all, I am grateful to Ruffin whose hard work has brought him his own rewards, to his father, James Magner, who hung in there, and to my parents, my mother, Jane Odil White, a teacher, and my late father, Thomas Boyett White, a life-long customer service engineer for IBM who provided essential financial support during Ruffin's early recovery from age three to six.

Dr. Ruffin White: Ruffin received his Bachelor of Science in Electrical Engineering from Rose-Hulman Institute of Technology, and his Masters in Computer Science from Georgia Tech. His doctoral research and dissertation "Usable Security and Verification for Distributed Robotic Systems" focused on cyber security for robots. While completing his PhD, Ruffin worked in Silicon Valley with nonprofit organizations to improve repeatability and reproducibility in robotic research and security using open source robotic software. He is currently founding an international tech startup to help commoditize his research for wider industry adoption. Ruffin has published to numerous scientific conferences and journals and is regularly invited to present for technical conventions globally.

A Short List of Recommended Reading:

Bernard Rimland, Ph.D., Navy psychologist, father of a son, Mark, *Infantile Autism: The Syndrome and Its Implications for a Neural Theory of Behavior*, (Century Psychology Series Award, 1962,) still in print, an award-winning classic, still readily available and updated nicely as to all the later science in a 50th anniversary edition.

Dorothy Beavers, Ph.D., chemist, mother of a son, Leo, *Autism: Nightmare Without End*, (Ashley Books 1981, 1982), long out of print, still available on Alibris.

Catherine Maurice, Ph.D. in French literature, mother of a daughter, Anne-Marie and a son, Michel, *Let Me Hear Your Voice*, (Knopf, 1993), still in print, and readily available.

Documentary Films:

Lövaas's classic 1987 video *Behavioral Treatment of Autistic Children*, now available on YouTube at https://www.youtube.com/watch?v=oGhIcAnBQZ4.

A two-minute trailer for an early forty-five-minute documentary film by Dr. Doreen Granpeesheh (Autism Society of America Professional of the Year) about Ruffin and three other recovered children, *Recovered: Journeys through the Autism Spectrum and Back*: https://www.youtube.com/watch?v=_tcJ1qO4je8

A one-minute trailer for a documentary film, *Recovering Ruffin*, focused solely on Ruffin available through Good Docs: https://gooddocs.net/products/recovering-ruffin

Mary Jane White is a poet and translator who practiced law at her home, the O. J. Hager House in Waukon, Iowa. She was born and raised in North Carolina, earned degrees from The North Carolina School of the Arts, Reed College, The University of Iowa Writers' Workshop, and studied law at Duke University, graduating from the University of Iowa. Her poetry and translations received NEA Fellowships in 1979 and 1985. She taught lyric poetry and poetry workshops briefly at the University of Iowa and at Luther College in Decorah, Iowa, and served for a decade as an Iowa Poet in the Schools, before her son, Ruffin, was born in 1991. She has been awarded writing scholarships to Bread Loaf (1979), Squaw Valley Community of Writers (2006), Bread Loaf Translators' Conference (2015), Writers in Paradise Conference (2016, 2018), Prague Summer Program for Writers (2017), Summer Literary Seminars in Tbilisi, Georgia (2018). Her first book, *Starry Sky to Starry Sky* (Holy Cow! Press, 1988), contains translations of Marina Tsvetaeva's long lyric cycle, "Miles," which first appeared in *The American Poetry Review* as an inserted feature. *After Russia: Poems by Marina Tsvetaeva* (Adelaide Books, New York/Lisbon, 2021) is her most recent translated work. Earlier poems and other translations have appeared widely across journals and magazines, have been included in various anthologies, and featured on Iowa Public Radio.

CPSIA information can be obtained
at www.ICGtesting.com
Printed in the USA
BVHW082018130422
634019BV00005B/12